Pendulum

Kylie Harrison

Pendulum

Poetic insights from a journey through mental illness

Pendulum: Poetic insights from a journey through mental illness
ISBN 978 1 74027 888 1
Copyright © text Kylie Harrison 2014
Cover: Erin Harrald

First published 2014
Reprinted 2016

Ginninderra Press
PO Box 3461 Port Adelaide SA 5015
www.ginninderrapress.com.au

Contents

Foreword	9
Introduction	11
Trauma	**13**
Trapped inside a coma	15
Blackness of the coma	16
In with silence	17
Clinging to life	18
Amnesia	**19**
Purpose	21
Amnesia	22
The white wall	23
Depression	**25**
In danger I play	28
Suffocating in darkness	29
Unplugged	30
Footsteps in the night	31
The trap of depression	33
Despairing in torment	34
The sea of melancholy	35
Mania	**37**
My brain thinks	39
Guinea pig escape/absconding from hospital	41
Pendulum	42
Psychosis	**43**
Alien psychosis	45
I am my illness	46
The man behind psychosis	47
Beyond delusion	48
Delusion is not the solution	49
Miscommunication	50

Dissociative parts	51
Night dictation	52
Holy Spirit's personal assistant	53
A distraction	54
Little tangents	55
Hallucination of a green angel	56
The comfort in voices	57
Reality transference	58
Psychosis – invasive pig	59
The secretary's journey	60
Sexual Trauma	**61**
Rain violation	63
Little black dress	64
The vulnerability of her illness	65
Stigma	**67**
The pain of stigma	69
Blamed for an illness	70
You are not to blame	71
Love and Friendship	**73**
Friends	75
Connection	76
As a sunset fades	77
Your gentle touch	78
Like a glove	79
Many future memories	80
Impulse of heart	81
Therapy	**83**
There is a way out	85
Clothed in shame	86
Forgiveness therapy	87
Freedom therapy	88
Purity therapy	89

Redecorate	90
Therapy through disassociation	91
Stability/Recovery	**93**
Poetry in a gum tree	95
A quiet crusade	96
A dolphin's world	97
Sky of dreams	98
In the midst of beauty	99
Giving lilies	100
Paradise in Cairns	101
Within the reach of safety	102
Through many tears	103
After the rain	104
Take one more step	105
Getting through	106
Broken instrument	107
Developing insight	108
Leave me alone	109
Who's to blame?	110
Symptom-free	111
Road to recovery	112
Chemical imbalance	113
Peer Work	**115**
Caring people	117
Walk in my shoes	118
Sharing a stepping stone	119
Roller coaster	120
Alteration	121
Walking through darkness	122
With a strong mind	123
Well-being can be restored	124
The rippling effect	125
The light in tomorrow	126

For my family, who have lived with bipolar disorder as long as I have, and my friends, including my boyfriend, for generating ideas and giving me the motivation to bring my vision to fruition.

I would like to acknowledge the support I have received from Jude Aquilina and a Richard Llewellyn Arts and Disability grant from the beginning of the project in 2011 until this exciting final stage. I would also like to thank Life Without Barriers.

Thank you to all the people in my life who have helped turn my grandiosity into a reality.

Foreword

Pendulum is an extraordinary collection of poetry. These hard-hitting poems could not have been written by anyone else but this highly creative, honest poet, film writer, stand-up comedian, peer support worker, writer and friend...Kylie Harrison.

I am privileged to have worked with Kylie on this book. Thanks to funding from the Richard Llewellyn Arts and Disability Trust, Kylie and I embarked on a poetry mentorship that lasted many years past the time frame and I know will continue.

Pendulum is one of those books that had to be written. Kylie always wrote poetry and kept journals. She wrote through her teens, through the onset of mental illness and into her adult life and present career as a peer support worker.

Kylie is the most inspirational speaker on mental health that I've heard. She speaks at schools and universities, to businesses and community groups. She speaks from the heart about her experiences and, in doing so, educates her audience and reduces stigma. It is little wonder the poems in *Pendulum* are emotive, edgy and extremely telling about what it is like to experience such states as psychosis or mania. Many poems reflect peaceful, happy times with family, friends or nature. Kylie is a keen observer of life, within and without – and a skilled portrayer of details: from the minute in the natural world, to the nuances of language affected by states of mind; from possible symbols to everyday miracles.

I invite you to climb aboard the big brass pendulum that

swings for us all and take a ride on one that sometimes goes a little higher and a little lower than most. Hold on tight when you reach the depths, but be assured this collection is inspiring and uplifting, as is the poet herself. *Pendulum* is an important debut poetry collection, as a contribution to Australian literature, as an educational tool for Kylie's public addresses, as a historical record and memoir, and as a study of mental health in the most powerful language of all – that of poetry.

Jude Aquilina

Introduction

I have written this book to reach out to the suffering, to give hope and comfort in the darkness, to help find resilience and motivation within the depression, to realise the illness is temporary and treatment is available. Knowing you don't want to stay where you are gives you the motivation to think about taking a step forward to persevere in the hard times, to reach out for support from loved ones or mentors in your life to give you encouragement, to feel less worthless and to have a purpose. Everyone has something only they can do. I know I am the only person who can write this book.

Before my job as a community peer worker, I volunteered in mental health services because I have a passion for standing up for the rights of people with mental illness who feel that they don't have a voice or that no one is listening. You can't find the light at the end of the tunnel unless you have walked in darkness for a while.

It's not only a matter of acknowledging where you stand but also discovering your potential and realising where you are going.

Trauma

… broken pendulum

At age fourteen, I was diagnosed with post-traumatic stress disorder and major depression. I went through a traumatic experience which triggered my illness. I nearly died and was airlifted from a country hospital to the city because I was in a coma and having seizures for two and a half hours.

I could hear my name being called.

'Kylie, wake up,' my mum seemed to shriek.

I struggled to answer her.

'Kylie, what's wrong? Please wake up. She's not responding. We need to get her to the hospital. We have to drive. It'll take ages for the ambos to come out here. Is she awake? Kylie. Kylie.'

I heard my name over and over again. What was wrong? I'm here, I kept saying. I'm here!

At some point I came to for a short time, heard the agonising noise of the helicopter, noticed the gas mask, felt the oxygen pouring into my lungs. I could hear the pandemonium of the air medical team.

Trapped inside a coma

Black-filled silence pierces my soul.
The absence of my heartbeat
creates a chaotic wave of intense terror.
I scream…to no avail.
Violent seizures wrestle within.
I confront death
just to see through the emptiness.

Blackness of the coma

With panic in my heart
I hear the urgent voice of the doctor.
There is a piercing silence
within the blackness of the coma.
There is a terrifying noise
as I hear the whir of a helicopter.

In with silence

I am in with the silence.
I am out with loudness.
I am shaking, with oxygen pumping.
These shocking noises make no sense
as I battle against brain failure.
I don't realise my body
is fighting a fight for my life.

Clinging to life

There was oxygen pumping
keeping me alive.
In terrifying silence
I waited

I thought I'd never wake up
but life beckoned me
like a canvas
to be painted.

Amnesia

… lost pendulum

I was in a coma. Everything was black. All that was left was my mind trying to understand, to grasp hold of anything. Realising I was probably dead forced me to start screaming in my mind. No one but God heard the piercing screech of the pain of seclusion from the world.

Please help me. I am not dead. Please hear me, please hear me, I said in my head.

I woke from the coma with amnesia. All I could recognise was my mother's voice. With my bipolar triggered, I would never be the same. My paranoia grew and I believed I was being punished in a prison, when in fact I was recovering in hospital.

How can I continue in a life I can't remember? How can I proceed when I can't remember how to walk? Lying endlessly imagining flashbacks of the trauma of the coma. Sleeping brings nightmares.

Purpose

There's something wrong
I don't understand.
Inside my mind I begin to cry.

Do I still have purpose on this earth?
I am weak, I can't talk
but I do not want to die.

What is left?
My brain is halved.
The question asked is Why?

Now I've found my breath
my heart's rhythm and my purpose
I could not say goodbye.

I sometimes live in doubt,
forget to trust.
Yet all I can do is try.

Amnesia

Fear pins me down.
I have amnesia,
but I am alive.
Strangers interrogate me.
Silence is my only answer.
I'm just trying to survive.

The white wall

I stare at the white wall.
Nothing left but emptiness.
I do not want to sleep
I don't know where I am.
The darkness comes
with shadows to torment me.
The white wall my only defence.

Depression

… pendulum swings low

When you are depressed, you might feel like you are in a pit or a deep hole that you can't get out of. Little do you know that within your reach is a ladder. But you are in complete darkness and cannot see it. This represents the services you can access but don't know about. When I found someone to help me, a torch was shone on the ladder and I could finally see my way out. Unfortunately, no one could actually help me out completely because I had to climb the ladder myself. I might only have the energy to climb one step but I know I have support to try two steps tomorrow. There are people believing in me at the top.

Recovery is a hard road but once I climbed a few steps I got more motivated and passionate to reach the top. To be honest, I was hanging onto these steps for thirty years before I made it to the top. I felt like I had climbed Mount Everest!

Sometimes when you are in that hole, no one comes. You can be alone. But, who knows, maybe there might be a ladder somewhere. Perhaps if you reach round your hole and try different services and treatments, you may find your way out too. My hope for you is that you will find the strength to reach out for help and find your own path to recovery. If you find yourself climbing down the ladder a few steps, don't worry, because you are no longer alone at the bottom. Don't worry about things you can't do, focus on what you can do.

I didn't know if I could do it but, with the right medication, the right treatment, which for me included ECT, along with the right psychiatrist and right therapy, the right support and strategies implemented, I found my road to recovery and I got to the top. Believe me, it took effort – it took nearly everything I had.

Sometimes I start to climb down the ladder as I start to develop symptoms again but I just hold on until I get the strength to climb back up again. Hopefully, I will never get to be at the bottom of that pit but I am now aware that if it happens I will have a ladder. I will seek treatment and support and will persevere to climb back to the top.

I know what the pit looks like now and recognise my early warning signs that lead me there and, with early intervention available now, I believe it is possible that I won't be at the bottom of the pit ever again, or at least I won't be alone.

I will continue to shine my torch as a peer worker; I can shine my light on the ladder because I've found it before. I can talk to support workers and mental health teams about the ladder's existence and can support the support worker to help the client. I can show the support worker how to shine a light on the ladder and encourage the support worker to encourage the client and believe that the client can get to the top. I know it was difficult to walk in the darkness – but I stumbled my way through believing there would be a light. Little did I know that one day I would be like a tour guide, leading others through the darkness to also find the light.

In danger I play

It may not be all it seems,
as sometimes I fall.
Yet I still remember my dreams,
so I get up and I crawl.

Wondering if anyone can hear,
longing for someone to reveal my quest,
heart racing, anxious with fear,
I cry out into the darkness.

I hope someone will take the burden away.
Perhaps it is my very own thorn.
I run and dance; in danger I play
but it was placed there before I was born.

Suffocating in darkness

My love, I cannot sleep for thinking of you.
How dismal to think of you drowning in melancholy.
Pounding abruptly, fierce and relentless,
despairing in torment, frantic to find energy again.

The sea of melancholy, the challenge, the fight,
all suffocate in darkness; you grope for any comfort,
desperate to be dragged from the cruel waves of melancholy.
Crushed, yet still determined to crawl toward my love.

Your body's weary, shamed, weak and terrified of failure.
But you can beat the disheartening wretchedness.
But the sea of melancholy will not overpower you;
those irrational fears will doubtlessly dissolve.

Determination and love – antagonists of melancholy –
will chance upon you and your desired happiness.
On stable ground you will again find comfort.
You're not deserted. I can be your strength.

My love, I cannot allow you to challenge the sea all alone.
Dearest, I cannot sleep for thinking of you.
Let us wade through the shallows till the dark water
leaves with the tide and we stand on sand again.

Unplugged

Sometimes it all feels meaningless.
Everything is affected.
It is hard to see through the emptiness
when your heart and head don't feel connected.

There's so much doubt in depression.
You tell me to search for the answers.
You tell me hope will show as my friend.
What is it that keeps me questioning,
longing for the doubt to end?

Footsteps in the night

1

Sit. Wait.
Watch the light flicker.
A chill. The harsh breeze
wraps her jacket tighter still.
A cobweb sways, dances ghost-like.

Look down.
There's slag on the ground,
potent stench of urine,
not a single soul to be found.
She is surrounded by an eyesore,
wrapped in a sea of graffiti.
A solitary tree has fallen
across train and tracks.
Oh, for such monstrosities:
the splendour of the trunk in ruin.
It had no protection, no defence
against its wretched enemy.

2

Sit. Wait
Watch the sudden glow
of a cigarette; hear footsteps
and an eerie cough.
Quick, fly like a moth.
Closer he comes,
faceless; he slurs his words,
his intention not quite clear.
Heavy load now a burden;
pace hastened by fear.
Frightened of his every move,
she hears yet another obscenity.

He loses his cloak of darkness.
She sees her escape opportunity.
Keys are found. Heart pounds.
Dark and silent inside her house.
Window found ajar.
Sneak quiet as a mouse.
Sit. Wait.

The trap of depression

Feeling so trapped, you can't get out.
And when the damage is done
you are locked in the deep dungeon,
alone, like the darkness has won.

Despairing in torment

I cannot sleep for thinking of you and what you do.
How dismal it must be, trapped, never feeling free,
as you pound abruptly, fierce and relentless,
desperate to be dragged from the cruel sea.

Despairing in torment, frantic to find energy again,
your irrational fears will be resolved.
You're not deserted; I can be your strength.
Together, this wretchedness will be dissolved.

The sea of melancholy

a sonnet

Sweet love, sleep not with dark sorrow this night;
do not despair, although the sea may stain.
The sea of melancholy, cruel to fight.
Alas, disheartened body, shamed with pain.
Anguish for fear of failure, desperate
to crawl elsewhere. Vanquish those doubts that cling.
Believe me, weary love, 'tis not too late;
take hold of this guidance I gently bring.
Your life, spirit and passion lost amid
irrational disturbing fears. Do not
allow the sea to wash away, to rid
yourself of happiness and all you've got.
Why do you act deserted and so alone?
Your faith? Believe the strength that I own.

Mania

… pendulum swings over the top

I became happy again – really happy to be out of the deep hole of depression. I was soon well enough to go back to school. The only problem was now I was too happy, laughing, making jokes and feeling euphoric. I started talking to anyone and everyone. Everything made me feel excited. This was the first time I experienced mania.

The teachers soon realised I wasn't well when I kept asking strange questions. I would interrupt the class and would start laughing at my own jokes in my head, when the class was silent.

No one understood me. I'd be laughing and next thing I'd be crying. I was having mood swings. I talked really fast and jumped from topic to topic, irrelevant to the subject. I'd only say half sentences because my brain was thinking so rapidly and, for the first time in my life, no one could understand me.

I can only do my best.

I envy those whose brains will rest.

My brain thinks

My brain thinks, too much I think,
but you don't know when to let go.
I've put up with you, been told what to do.
A whispering whirlwind, my brain thinks that's you.

My brain thinks, too much I think.
Too much to bear, as they refuse to care.
How hard I have fought without their support.
Surely they know the rivers I've wept.
Why didn't anyone intercept?

My brain thinks, too much I think. Can't remember things
I've said, or understand the rapid patterns in my head.
What I need, I just can't get. My confusion makes me upset.
My brain thinks it's about to pop;
I scream inside for the torment to stop.

My brain thinks, too much I think.
My actions now seem to repel,
so I often walk alone in this world.
The wall too high and too wide,
thinking no one would care if I died.
My brain thinks it can't take any more,
I could leave the loneliness
and walk through the last dark door.

My brain thinks, too much I think.
Trapped inside a deep dark pit,
I struggle to find worth in it.
Anger and doubt fill my heart;
my brain's on alert to play some part.
Insanity troubles my body so wretched,
sorrow and pain creates a life rejected.

My brain thinks, too much I think.
But you don't know when to let go.
I've put up with you, been told what to do.
A whispering whirlwind, my brain thinks that's you.

My brain thinks too much, I think.
I can only do my best.
I envy those whose brains will rest.

My brain thinks,
too much I think.
My brain thinks,
too much I think.

Guinea pig escape/absconding from hospital

As the fog cleared, we heard
the hum and chant of thistles.
Our watered mouths
devoured the wet leaves.
We danced among the stalks
and squealed with rapture.
Alarmed by a thump behind us,
we raced between stems,
scurried and squealed,
with the grim idea of being caught.
We dodged the eager hands
of those who'd hoped to lure us back
to that darkened cage,
that cold place –
our habitat and existence.

And there in the hum and chant of thistles
we built our homes and made our beds.
We escaped our wire cells
as we dashed further
than their hands could search
and found our freedom.

Pendulum

Swinging only slightly at first.
Higher, then lower. Higher, lower.
Gaining speed; showing intense feelings,
crying out for the swing to go slower.

Dangerous speeds, out of control.
Close to death, want to get free.
Swing with strength one step further,
my weakness visible for all to see.

Crying louder, want to get off.
With nothing left, I am flung through the air.
Soaring through the empty darkness,
my mind and heart begin to tear.

Flying gracefully through deep problems
unaware of the sadness in reality;
laughing and soaring into the heavens,
knowing not of the danger and hidden cruelty.

Euphoria and delight spring from my heart.
Pendulum's force no longer a fight.
Whatever I do, I do no wrong
for now in my head things feel just right.

Pendulum swings dangerously, wipes out my smile.
Why is it that, now, things feel all wrong?
The pendulum up and pendulum down.
Despite everything, I must remain strong.

Understanding without control;
the determined pendulum may never still.
I can't get off when I've been put back on.
It is my reality to face the pendulum's will.

Psychosis

… tangled pendulum

When I cannot face the stress or trauma in reality, my brain takes over so I do not have to feel the pain, and I go into my own dimension where I am confident nothing can hurt me, like heaven on earth, my own la-la land where I am temporarily relieved of responsibility and believe my purpose is what the dissociative parts in my psychosis are telling me.

When I am psychotic, I feel like I stop thinking and someone is in control of what I say, think or do. I gradually lose reality and this is really scary when I have insight to know what is happening. I begin to experience distorted thinking; paranoid that people are after me or I am in a game and everyone is against me. Psychosis says to me, KYLIE IS GONE. YOUR NEW NAME IS TRINITY! YOU ARE THE HOLY SPIRIT'S SECRETARY.

Trinity is like a six-year-old. Trinity is a dissociative part in psychosis.

Trinity trusts everyone, does not have boundaries, does not understand sexual connotations or advances, loves attention, wants to please everyone, on a mission to save the world. Little girl with no fear, hitch-hikes and jumps into the passenger seat of strangers' cars, thinks everyone is a holy person sent by God.

Alien psychosis

I'm an alien.
I surely must be;
why else would I be green?

I'm Jesus Christ.
I'm almost certain that's right;
I've known this my whole life.

My name is Trinity.
I'd like to be addressed as such,
although some people call me Kylie.

I'm the Holy Spirit's secretary.
That I truly must be,
for I write and write continually.

I'm an alien.
I surely must be;
why else would I be green?

I am my illness

I am severe
within my stillness.
I think I need to save the world.
I am my illness.

Challenge him,
but you won't win.
It's no longer fair;
psychosis has got in.

Next will be a silence;
across my mouth he'll put some tape.
With me bound, he's in control –
psychosis plans his escape.

I am getting sicker.
More talking in my head.
Voices becoming angry.
I'm sacrificed instead.

I am severe
within my stillness.
I think I need to save the world.
I am my illness.

The man behind psychosis

Condemnation.
Psychosis.
Thoughts invading mine.

Man in black clothes,
black sunglasses
thinks he's God's gift to women.

Swapping from personality to personality.
Out to prove he can do anything.
He's in control.

She listens anxiously.
Detaches from her feelings,
laughs and rejects responsibility.

She feels paralysed and numb.
In her silliness, he shows his authority.
He is in control.

Beyond delusion

I like the illusion
that I am forced to steal.
Is it all a delusion?
Is my world not real?

I get lost in confusion,
don't know right from wrong.
People create disillusion
when I'm no longer strong.

Delusion is not the solution

I'm in a game. Everyone's against me.
I'm on the lookout for confirmation,
trying to discover what is real,
finding paranoia and hallucination.

Does it matter what side I'm on,
reality or delusion?
No matter how hard I try,
my brain cannot find a solution.

I'm laughing through my pain,
I'm angry that I can't cry.
What is wrong with me, I say.
This struggle within me… Why?

Along the journey to recovery
too many obstacles cause me tension.
The roller coaster plays with me
as I struggle with my perception.

But I no longer give up easily
as I am taught how to fight.
Now I search for safety,
knowing that it's my right.

Miscommunication

When my world is full of distortion
and there is poor communication,
when things get blown out of proportion,
I seek positive affirmation.

Dissociative parts

Like peas in a pod,
we clamber together.
Moods jumping,
dissociate parts flying.
Ever changing
like the weather,
one day longing for love,
next, my faith is dying.

Night dictation

A promotion had been planned;
it's no longer in the distance.
I was the Holy Spirit's secretary,
now give him personal assistance.

In the middle of the night,
it's all done by negotiation.
I can't have my own thoughts
as I obediently take down dictation.

Holy Spirit's personal assistant

I am no longer the Holy Spirit's secretary;
a promotion is on the way.
I am now his personal assistant.
I want the voice to stay.

I'm on a special mission –
the prophecy's fulfilled.
It's only a voice inside my head;
my purpose is yet to be revealed.

A distraction

Psychosis constantly harasses her,
in the third person
tormenting her,
forcing her out.

Crying and screaming,
seeks direction but can't listen.
Until medication steps in
to let in a distraction.

Little tangents

She's trying to help.
She wants to be quiet.
She goes off on her own little tangents,
not careful of what she says,
aware she can be misinterpreted.
When she tries to be quiet,
psychosis struggles within her.
She reacts involuntarily,
responding to her voices.
She goes off on her own little tangents.

Hallucination of a green angel

Staring at the sun
tears rolling down my cheeks
longing to see glorious colours
as a white angel radiates green.
The cemetery a golden cross
reveals more in this heavenly scene.
Staring helplessly through the tears…
Can others see this, or is it just for me?

The comfort in voices

Sometimes the voices comfort him.
He has friends every hour of every day.
Sometimes they are mean to him;
he says that's the price he has to pay.

Sometimes they are angry,
with a commanding tone.
Yet if he didn't have his voices,
he says he would feel alone.

Reality transference

Reality transference
within the torment of illness
mysterious and life-giving.
A moment to be recognised
as you strive for your best.
A moment to be remembered
as a victory against psychosis.

Psychosis – invasive pig

Shut up. Get lost.
Stay away from my brain.
You tell me I'm guilty,
that we are just the same.

I'm not you, psychosis,
and I never wanted to be.
You're in a class of your own,
and you will also see
that I'm smarter than you know.
I've learned your tricks,
your party games.

I know almost all of your ways.
You are an invasive pig.
Get out of my brain.
You tell me I'm guilty,
but we are not the same.

The secretary's journey

Thoughts are mercilessly invaded.
A third person talks about you.
You have no control
over what you say, think or do.

Your mind is being ridiculous
but it all seems especially true.
You cannot see the irony.
You are not Jesus – you are you.

Suddenly a six-year-old appears;
Trinity has arrived.
Your mind in a childlike state;
through trauma, you survived.

Psychosis is a secret maze.
The Holy Spirit's secretary is there.
She files away your pain.
She is the only one to care.

When the mind is better,
Trinity is nowhere to be found.
She's gone to her safe place.
Laughter is now her crown.

Sexual Trauma

… pendulum abused

When someone is psychotic they are extremely vulnerable and can be easily led. Many people in this position can be taken advantage of. It is more likely that someone who is psychotic will become a victim of assault, rather than the perpetrator of crime.

I was sixteen years old. As I got out the car and thanked the motorist, he warned me how dangerous hitch-hiking was. He put his hand on my knee and said, 'Listen, love, in future do not get in the car with a bastard like me.'

I suffered post-traumatic stress disorder because of the abuse and sexual assault I endured during manic episodes. When I am unwell, I often hitch-hike or jump into strangers' cars. Obviously I am greatly at risk in this state of mind. I have been really lucky sometimes, others not so lucky.

I suffered with PTSD for five years, suffering insomnia, flashbacks and nightmares of an incident. Things I saw would trigger anxiety. I would suddenly be reminded of the incident and would have panic attacks as if it was happening again. It is frightening to keep reliving something you really want to forget. I got down to a size 6 as I wasn't eating. Self-harm and suicidal thoughts arose and PTSD caused me to attempt an overdose.

As I had severe PTSD, it was ECT (shock treatment) which helped me…there was memory loss involved, which actually really helped. It became more of a distant memory instead of feeling like I was constantly reliving it.

Rain violation

He held her tight,
fondled her breasts,
stroked her hair;
her face he kissed.

Her mouth he grasped.
She pleaded in pain;
her screams were faint,
vanquished by the rain.

Despite her protests
he forced her to stay.
Beyond her control –
he went all the way.

Little black dress

Ready for a big night out –
a sexy, short little black dress,
make-up and high heels.
Certainly dressed to impress.

Later I cried
at the fire I lit,
the night everything changed.
Was I asking for it?

To destroy the memory –
a harsh lesson to learn,
as I tearfully watch fragments
of the black dress burn.

The vulnerability of her illness

When her rights are lost and misused
injustice marches through the door
and she cannot escape from being abused.

Stigma

… pendulum stained

The stigma surrounding mental illness can be so strong. It places a wall of silence around the issue. The effects are damaging to the community and to the person with the illness, their friends and family.

Growing up in a country town, primary school was great, as I had lots of friends, did heaps of sport and loved music. I loved learning and was the school captain in Year 7. At high school, things were different. I got harassed constantly. I got a reputation for being rebellious because I was hitch-hiking at night. I was branded a psycho by some of the boys. They constantly paid me out. It went round the town that I was going to a mental hospital and I felt deserted by even my closest friends.

I could have had a plaque near my grave but instead I have a plaque across my forehead that reads 'mentally unwell'.

Sometimes when I get really enthusiastic in my job, I say I am trying to eradicate stigma. If only it was as easy as eradicating bugs. If only people in society as a whole were supportive, empathetic and less judgemental.

The pain of stigma

My illness turned me against my mate
yet he never tried to investigate.
The name, the illness, the pain
broke my heart and confused my brain.
I did get better, but he refused to wait.

Blamed for an illness

Why are we blamed for an illness?
Acceptance is not a new discovery.
How hard is it to stand beside us
As we strive to find recovery?

Does a mother deliver her own baby?
Why do we have to suffer on our own?
All we need is someone to care, to listen.
You can't fight the war in your head alone.

You are not to blame

Try not to be so hard on yourself.
You can be your own worst enemy.
You're allowed to get it wrong sometimes.
You take on too much responsibility.

The stigma remains;
ignorance is revealed.
It's not your fault
for the shame that you feel.

Some things can be different.
It won't always be the same.
The problem is the problem.
You are not to blame.

Love and Friendship

… pendulum cherished

I needed to hear my mum's voice. I loved hearing my mum read. She is very expressive and reading was her forte. She read to me so I could hear her voice; I couldn't understand the book at all, but, hearing my mum's voice, I knew I was still alive.

But what actually brought me out of my melancholy was quite remarkable. My sister Erin started tickling me.

I was kind of annoyed at first and weakly said, 'Don't.'

I heard Mum say, 'Keep doing it. She's responding.'

Don't, I thought, but suddenly her tickles had me laughing involuntarily. She kept doing it and I started laughing for real and suddenly recognised my sister.

Cry out for help and someone will listen. Someone will send you a floatie until you get rescued. Believe. Have faith: know you are being listened to, that people care you are suffering.

Friends

Some friends are like building blocks
while others are like gates with locks.

Some friends are like playing cards
while others are like security guards.

Some friends are like never-ending tours
while others are like revolving doors.

Connection

Burning like an amber coal,
your passion ignites my soul.
Each time I look into your eyes,
I search, but can find no lies.

To be your friend, to walk by your side,
a connection is felt, I cannot deny,
as I catch a glimpse of your smile
a twinkle I hadn't seen in a while.

Burning like an amber coal,
your passion ignites my soul.
Each time I look into your eyes,
my heart fills up with butterflies.

Blazing like the afternoon sun,
I realise I am not the only one.
As I watch the sun set on this day,
my thoughts just silently fade away.

As a sunset fades

An exquisite summer sunset
described nothing of their love:
the way he held her against his body,
the way hers trembled at his touch.
A thousand sparkling stars
described nothing of his kiss;
nothing compared to their devotion.
They longed to be close day and night,
thought their love would never fade.
Yet without notice life changed.

An exquisite summer sunset
now describes something of their love.
It was there for a moment,
then disappeared into darkness.
He can no longer touch her,
hold her or kiss her,
nor see her beauty again.
He stumbles along the beach,
stares helpless at the romantic sight.
An exquisite summer sunset
grasps him hard by the heart.

Your gentle touch

My moist mouth longs for your lips,
to tenderly caress, to meet with mine.
Your kiss is like a thousand compliments,
each more gentle and sweet than the first.
I know your lips are both charming and true,
enchanting me like the beckoning sea.

I yearn for your forthright love
and desire to share in the passion.
As I quietly listen to the sound of your voice,
hormones explode within my patient inner being.

I want your powerful arms to pull me close,
to hold me, and fingers to stroke my hair,
When you press your muscular body against me,
mine quivers like a leaf dances in the wind.

Investigating every inch of your sweet body,
caressing skin as love draws us together.
To be near you, to see you smile,
I feel treasured and precious.

There's style in your gentle touch
which makes me feel like a sexy goddess.
Fascinated by your alluring charm,
my spirit races, longing for your love,
for the warmth you offer with tenderness,
and I thirst to give you back the pleasure.

Like a glove

If I were cold,
you'd be like my glove.
I love your warm heart.
I treasure your love.

Many future memories

In my exploration,
to find respect that is strong,
I found a thoughtful friend,
so things wouldn't be as wrong.

When I sought your friendship,
I also found spontaneity.
You offered me your attention
but found me not in your reality.

Even though you couldn't understand me,
as manic I was too,
there are many future memories
I want to share with you.

Impulse of heart

Sweet love, no logical explanation
could possibly explain gentle desire.
It's either there or it's futile; reason
cannot control a force as wild as fire.
Compassion, my beloved, is valour.
You make me laugh when all is sorrowful.
This love you give could never be truer;
it is more precious than a buried jewel.
Is there something more worthy to esteem
than that of love? A longing to be held
and treasured, isn't it like a breathless dream?
Does not pure love add beauty to our world?
Unconquerable is the impulse of heart.
This force is strong, a soul's essential part.

Therapy

… pendulum swings upwards

Anyone who has tried a few different medications has probably felt like a guinea pig. It might feel like nothing is working but it is like walking on a tightrope. Sometimes, medication can be like the safety net. There are many medications. I have found the right medication for me after fifteen years. I never thought I would be able to work and could not even imagine I could live this well.

After finding the right medication, I did some therapy with my psychiatrist that I call trauma therapy. It is a journey of visualisation. Once in a session, I visualised myself with all the negative memories and grabbed a sledgehammer and smashed them to pieces. I found it empowering.

In my visualisation therapy with my psychiatrist, I first saw visions of a wall. This wall was black and it was called the overcoming wall, in contrast to the white wall. It represented my fear of the blackness. I visualised the door opening to a magical land with rainbows and waterfalls. I have written poetry about this place – my safe place. In this therapy, I find purity, forgiveness and freedom. I see visions and my spirit and subconscious experience amazing things. My mind is transformed and the long process of healing is complete.

In my therapy, I let go of all that was not important. All the bad stuff was smashed to pieces and I have been set free, feel rejuvenated and alive again.

In the end of my dissociation therapy, my dissociate parts, including Trinity, decide to remain in my safe place and release me to just be Kylie.

There is a way out

You beat yourself up
blame yourself,
put yourself in prison.
The key is there
but you don't allow yourself
to walk out the door.

You've been there so long,
feeling paralysed,
you've forgotten
you can turn the key.

Clothed in shame

Sweet love,
you are my precious pearl.
What happened to you
still gives me pain.

I saw your suffering –
not forgiving yourself,
clothing yourself in shame,
when there is nothing to forgive.

Forgiveness therapy

To think of the hurt,
the injustice, the pain.
He is guilty, a criminal.
He deserves the blame.

The unfairness of the crime.
Is judgement fair?
He should pay for wrongdoing,
yet remorse is rare.

'Let him go,' I cry,
although it doesn't make sense.
Why give him freedom?
He didn't pay for his offence.

I am in the prison,
the victim trapped within,
but forgiveness must be found
or the wicked will always win.

Freedom therapy

Soaring together on an eagle,
flying over a stunning city.
We're little children playing a game,
the reward of being set free.

Purity therapy

I am wearing a white dress,
shimmering with jewels.
I stand near a lake,
admiring the waterfalls.

I am safe in this garden
and I want to stay.
It is a precious secret refuge,
refreshing the scars of yesterday.

Redecorate

Within this beautiful place,
are enormous positives to gain:
exhilarating glimpses within my heart,
precious memories that will remain.

When you are going through hard times,
try to recapture the mystery,
to dwell on pretty times –
redecorate your history.

Through my journey to recovery
I found friends along the way.
This is what I will treasure most:
memories locked in my heart to stay.

Therapy through disassociation

When the mind is better,
Trinity is nowhere to be found.
She's gone to the safe place;
from her lips there's no more sound.

Her voices do not stay;
dissociative parts dissolve at last.
She has found strategies to cope.
They are now buried in her past.

Stability/Recovery

… pendulum finds a steady rhythm

Learning early warning signs and gaining insight I now see as some of my greatest accomplishments. To me, it's not so much an illness – but a *challenge*!

There should be psychiatrists, nurses, key workers, support workers and peer workers working together. There needs to be an effective team environment, with the consumer directing the decisions. Peer workers have experienced pain and suffering, have experienced being patient with the system, have experienced frustration, anger and stigma.

Sometimes on my journey towards recovery, I have run with leaps and bounds. Sometimes I have walked or even crawled, but there have been so many times in my life when I have said, 'Please carry me, for I cannot take one more step.'

The best advice I ever received was when I was nineteen, and was given to me by my mother. She said, 'Your illness is not your fault, but it is your responsibility.'

I have an analogy about how my family treats me. I compare myself to my brother's BMWs. One is constantly breaking down and one is perfect. I tell my brother I am like the BMW that keeps breaking down, but he always treats me like the perfect BMW!

Recovery to me is being part of the team and discovering a pathway through the unknown, to rediscover a certainty or reality within the delusion, some insight amongst the chaos and finding understanding as a solution of how to control the roller coaster of emotions.

Poetry in a gum tree

With the birds chirping,
the breeze against my skin,
I sit in my gum tree.
I'm happy, full of awe,
gazing at the clouds.
With creation surrounding me,
I feel safe, I feel secretive,
as I write my poetry.

A quiet crusade

Linger over Queen and Knight,
Eye the Bishop, ready to fight.
Castles enclose from where they stand,
Pawns prepare to foil a plan.
Queen swiftly advances toward hesitant King,
Defence sends Queen and Knight from distant wing.
Bishop follows, eager to inspect,
Defence is captured in an unexpected check.
This battle has a quiet charm
As there is no actual hurt or harm.
If only all battles of such contest
Were innocent as a game of chess.

A dolphin's world

I am swimming and giggling with the sea,
hoping for someone to play with me.
I see a boat and beam with delight,
I do turns and show how great I can be.
Diving beneath the deep blue sea,
I discover the wreckage underneath me.
Those sunken boats left to sleep silently,
pieces of wood and metal shaped exquisitely.
Coral and seaweed and rocks as far as I can see,
schools of fish swimming happily.
This is my world, this deep blue sea.
This is where I feel completely free.

Sky of dreams

Gazing dreamily at the misty sky,
watching the clouds, not asking why.
Amid the colours of an autumn night,
I can't help but stare at the perfect sight
while the ripples of waves gently reflect
the peace and warmth like a soft blanket.

In the midst of beauty

The colours of a bitter winter night
weave together and make an inspiring sight.
Each time a new sunset pattern is born;
every night a perfect picture is drawn.

Giving lilies

Sharing lilies.
Giving blessings.
Delight in their colour,
the abundance of greatness,
soft brilliance and excellence.
Memories lasting,
of people caring.
When sickness prevailed
lilies spoke of hope.

Paradise in Cairns

Within clear sands and pocket-sized huts,
there is murky water and hidden crocs.
A harvest of concealed coconuts:
still life beneath forgotten rocks.

Palm trees sway in the breeze.
Over mossy rocks a waterfall cascades.
I long to stay, I never want to leave.
Within this beauty, a problem fades.

Within the reach of safety

How pleasurable life would be
if I could reach out for safety,
letting go as if I could fly,
soaring and bidding sorrow goodbye.

Through many tears

Clinging in desperation,
paralysed with fears.
Everyone needs inspiration
that's found through many tears.

Think before you climb the ladder.
I won't lie; it can be tough.
Maybe at first you will feel sadder –
remember, one step will be enough.

Keep moving, don't remain inactive.
Thoughts will need to be rearranged.
You can succeed if you're proactive.
Your circumstances can be changed.

After the rain

Sometimes life is tough.
Many times I've thought, 'That's enough.'

Hoping for hope,
when I feel I can't cope.

Yet after the rain clouds go,
there often appears a radiant rainbow.

Take one more step

At times I have nothing but bad memories;
often I don't have what I require.
Now and again I run, then I walk,
yet sometimes I feel my vitality is on fire.

When I simply cannot take one more step,
I then realise I have some more to give.
Laughing and talking with family and friends
gives me peace and a purpose to live.

Getting through

How can you trust again
when it feels like everyone is against you?
Some will beat their wounded,
yet that's not the worst they'll do.

Concentrate on what is good,
focus on things that are true.
Believe in yourself and find hope;
your friends will get you through.

Broken instrument

Even if you're the best musician,
you'll never go on tour
if you play with a broken instrument –
your performance will be poor.

The brain is so complicated.
It is a challenge to find insight.
If your brain is a broken instrument,
you'll find it hard to tune it right.

As your brain is being repaired,
it's time for motivation.
Realise your responsibility,
with practice and determination.

Developing insight

Sitting at a coffee shop
watching the crowds flowing.
Tourists have maps,
locals know where they're going.

At first you are like a tourist;
mental illness just appears.
You don't know the patterns;
you try to follow a map for years.

Slowly you develop insight,
your understanding is rare.
You no longer need a map,
you remember how you got there.

Leave me alone

No matter what I do, I do no wrong,
yet in my head your thoughts are strong.
You have no right to control me;
stay away from me and my head.
With medication, you'll soon be dead.

Who's to blame?

Who's to blame for my pain?
When it's hot, I wait for the rain.
In the darkness I crawl along.
Will someone help me to be strong?

Fire raging within my heart,
breathless, I watch my team do their part.
Sunshine rising, yet another day,
blessings pouring down on me in every way.
Who's to blame for my pain?
Not I, but it is my responsibility just the same.

Symptom-free

In my heart there was a longing,
a yearning to be treasured:
to be set free from my mood swings.
The struggle could not be measured.

The right medication has been found
after so much perseverance.
Holding on tight to the goal,
to live my rescue plan of resilience.

I take my medication as prescribed;
now I live a life symptom-free.
With strategies, I'm in control;
the roller coaster now listens to me.

Road to recovery

Anyone can be on the road to recovery.
There can be a rainbow after the rain,
no matter how hard it seems,
however deep the pain.

Challenge today, to exceed expectations.
Believe you will stand tall.
Be strong to find your essence.
Build a bridge that will not fall.

Chemical imbalance

Distant memories of a mind twisted,
suddenly a mood is lifted:
sadness, buried where children play,
covering scars of yesterday.

Chemicals that dance:
stability by chance –
the possibility of stillness
beyond my mental illness.

Peer Work

… pendulum shines and reflects

I began my job as a community peer worker five years ago and I was originally employed by Life Without Barriers as a trainee peer worker. It was an amazing opportunity for me, since I hadn't been able to work for years and had lived on a disability pension for most of my life. The opportunity to become employed and earn an income was something I'd previously thought impossible. I am fortunate to attempt to reduce stigma by doing presentations in the community, supporting colleagues and clients with my lived experience and facilitating group activities.

I believe if I inspire even just one person to want to live, all the pain and suffering will have been worth it. Without the pain and suffering I have had to endure, I would not be the same person I am today.

I have made a number of digital stories and short films that you can watch on my website kylieharrison.wordpress.com.

I made a digital story called *Rippling Effect* to show where my journey of mental illness began and how I found recovery. I was a part of the Cracking Up mental health stand-up comedy group and I performed my own comedy show at the Mercury Cinema in Mental Health Week 2012. I have received grants from the Richard Llewellyn Art and Disability Trust to support me to write this poetry book and do stand-up comedy. All these projects are about my lived experience with mental illness.

We need to work together to build a community where people are listened to, people are respected and valued, people have independence, experience freedom and are allowed to discover their own empowerment.

Caring people

A place to belong,
friendships to make,
love to be shared,
people who give, not just take.

Life Without Barriers –
now what can I say?
These caring people
support you all of the way.

Walk in my shoes

As I tell my story,
you spend five minutes in my head.
Walk a while in my shoes –
reflect on things I've said.

Sharing a stepping stone

Telling people I get sick
can be like a stepping stone.
As I share with others,
I find out I'm not alone.

Together we can take some steps.
There is a way across this stream
and maybe we can't make it
until we are a team.

Roller coaster

Be ready for the roller coaster.
Don't allow him to trick you.
Psychosis will return,
yet it is possible to ride it through.

He knows the journey like no one else.
He causes maximum distress.
As part of the team we must stop him –
won't let the roller coaster progress.

Alteration

I search for compassion,
beyond devastation.
In every situation
hope brings transformation.

Walking through darkness

Although I've walked in darkness,
it seems I have no choice.
It appears I am talking to myself,
yet people are following my voice.

Although I walk in darkness
and I don't know if my path is right,
I don't realise I am like a tour guide,
leading others toward the light.

With a strong mind

Acknowledging consequence
will eventually make sense.
With diligent perseverance,
you can make a difference.

Well-being can be restored

I'm not so much exposing myself;
it is my illness I'm revealing.
With stepping stones leading to recovery,
hearts and minds will begin believing.

Sometimes all we need is reassurance,
resilience and a high expectation.
Guarding our minds against intruder thoughts
to quietly accept our situation.

People can learn from their mistakes.
Some voices need to be ignored.
Change is about moving forward.
Health and well-being can be restored.

The rippling effect

Have you ever wondered
what a difference can be made?
Do something to help someone,
and that memory will never fade.

In my job I speak about mental illness,
share with honesty what I've been through.
It is our job to combat stigma.
It's up to me and it's up to you.

When I share with the community,
I am an expert in my field.
I believe in a rippling effect across the water,
and in the strength of the bridge I build.

We need to open up;
more knowledge brings us wealth.
There is a hidden expertise
in the lived experience of mental health.

No matter what you've been through
there are ways of learning to cope.
Accept yourself and your strength,
for I believe there is always hope.

The light in tomorrow

A place of comfort
within the sorrow.
Enjoying every moment,
I now can't wait for tomorrow.

www.ingramcontent.com/pod-product-compliance
Lightning Source LLC
Chambersburg PA
CBHW070918080526
44589CB00013B/1348